GETTING
IN THE GAP

Other Hay House Books by Dr Wayne W. Dyer

All of the above are available at your local bookstore, or may be ordered by visiting:
Hay House UK: www.hayhouse.co.uk; **Hay House USA:** www.hayhouse.com®;
Hay House Australia: www.hayhouse.com.au; **Hay House South Africa:** www.hayhouse.co.za;
Hay House India: www.hayhouse.co.in

GETTING
IN THE GAP

Making Conscious Contact with God Through Meditation

Dr Wayne W. Dyer

HAY HOUSE

Carlsbad, California • New York City • London • Sydney
Johannesburg • Vancouver • Hong Kong • New Delhi

First published and distributed in the United Kingdom by:
Hay House UK Ltd, Astley House, 33 Notting Hill Gate, London W11 3JQ
Tel: +44 (0)20 3675 2450; Fax: +44 (0)20 3675 2451
www.hayhouse.co.uk

Published and distributed in the United States of America by:
Hay House Inc., PO Box 5100, Carlsbad, CA 92018-5100
Tel: (1) 760 431 7695 or (800) 654 5126
Fax: (1) 760 431 6948 or (800) 650 5115
www.hayhouse.com

Published and distributed in Australia by:
Hay House Australia Ltd, 18/36 Ralph St, Alexandria NSW 2015
Tel: (61) 2 9669 4299; Fax: (61) 2 9669 4144
www.hayhouse.com.au

Published and distributed in the Republic of South Africa by:
Hay House SA (Pty) Ltd, PO Box 990, Witkoppen 2068
Tel/Fax: (27) 11 467 8904
www.hayhouse.co.za

Published and distributed in India by:
Hay House Publishers India, Muskaan Complex, Plot No.3, B-2,
Vasant Kunj, New Delhi 110 070
Tel: (91) 11 4176 1620; Fax: (91) 11 4176 1630
www.hayhouse.co.in

Distributed in Canada by:
Raincoast Books, 2440 Viking Way, Richmond, B.C. V6V 1N2
Tel: (1) 604 448 7100; Fax: (1) 604 270 7161; www.raincoast.com

A catalogue record for this book is available from the British Library.

ISBN: 978-1-78180-498-8

Printed and bound in Great Britain by
TJ International, Padstow, Cornwall.

For my daughter
Serena Joanna Dyer.
Your loving smiling spirit lights up
every space you enter.

Contents

*"Through the rise and fall of empires, through the creation
of vast bodies of symbols that give shape to our dreams;
through the forging of magic keys with which to unlock
the mysteries of creation . . . through it all we are
marching from epoch to epoch towards the fullest
realization of our soul.*

*"Yes, we are coming, the pilgrims, one and all—
coming to our true inheritance of the world,
we are ever broadening our consciousness,
ever seeking a higher and higher unity;
ever approaching nearer to the one universal truth
which is the All—comprehensive all embracing."*

— Rabindranath Tagore, 1861–1941

Introduction

The gap is an exquisite place! It's a place where miracles occur. The gap is owned by everyone on this planet. It's yours to enter at will. What awaits you in the gap is the experience of activating the higher human dimensions of insight, intuition, creativity, and peak performance; as well as coming to know relaxation, enchantment, bliss, and the peace of making conscious contact with God.

As you begin reading this short book and listening to the meditation download that accompanies it and begin the practice of going into the gap, keep uppermost in your mind that you can enter this glorious gap between your thoughts at any moment you choose. (Download instructions are at the end of this book, after the transcript.) The power of the gap is available to you in the midst of a business meeting, at the dinner table while engaged in a heated discussion, on the 18th tee of a long day on the golf course, or even while riding on a crowded bus.

You own the gap! No one can take it from you, and the doorway into the gap is always unlocked and available to you. Once you master the techniques for entering the gap, you'll find yourself seeking out the wondrous energies of this miraculous place frequently. No one will even know that in the quagmire of a horrendous traffic jam where everyone around you is steeped in frustration and anxiety, you've dismissed them all and have chosen the serenity of the gap, if only for a moment. Doing so will reinvigorate your soul and remind you to be in a state of appreciation rather than depreciation. You've left the mob of people who are looking at this moment as an occasion to be offended, and have entered the gap where you're now using it to be in a state of peace. Such is the value of knowing how to slip into the gap at will with a few short internal mental images.

The gap will teach you how to listen like you've never listened before. Now take the letters that make up the word *listen* and rearrange them so that they spell out *silent*. *listen/silent—listen/silent*—the same in content only arranged to appear different from each other. When you listen, you'll feel the silence. When you're silent, you'll hear at a new level of listening. Try it in the gap, then begin to apply it in all of your interactions. Listen with silence. Note that the word *silence* and the word *license* also have the exact same letters as well. Silence gives you a license to listen and be silent simultaneously. By going into the gap and using the methods suggested here in this work, you'll come to treasure the space between your thoughts. For it's in this silent space called the gap that you'll come to make conscious contact with God. I send you love and peace as you begin this journey.

—Wayne W. Dyer

"What is at work during inner silence

is another faculty that man has,

the faculty that makes him a magical being . . ."

— don Juan Matus

Chapter One

Why Meditate?

Why meditate? Anyone reading this book has at one time or another considered this question and come up with all sorts of answers. Some of the many reasons for meditating include reducing stress, cultivating a sense of peace, eliminating fatigue, slowing the aging process, improving memory, finding clarity of purpose, and even healing. All of these are powerful motivators for beginning a meditation practice. Who wouldn't want the healthy, happy, and purposeful life that is the result of these benefits?

However, all these reasons pale in significance to the real-ization that *meditation is our way of making conscious contact with God.*

The paramount reason for making meditation a part of our daily life is to join forces with our sacred energy and regain the power of our Source (God). Through meditation, we can tap in to an abundance of creative energy that resides within us, and a more meaningful experience of life, which enriches us permanently. By meditating, we come to *know* God rather than *know about* God. However, before we can make the shift to a more enriching life, we have to tame our ego.

Taming the Ego

What is ego? Essentially, it's an idea that we carry around with us about who we really are. We all have an ego, and it's quite useful at times, but given the upper hand, it disconnects us from God. Most of us personalize our ego with some of the following thoughts:

I am what I do.
I am what I have.
I am separate from God.
I am what others think of me.
I am separate from everyone else.
I am separate from what is missing in my life.

Sometime during our life, we identified ourselves as variations of these six beliefs. Our physical body became the means for identifying ourselves as distinct from others. Possessions, achievements, and reputation became our calling cards. Things we believed were missing became goals. This aspect of ourselves is what I am calling *ego*. We need to tame the ego so that we can regain our all-encompassing source of power.

Our sense of empowerment is diminished when we identify solely with the ego, whose main concern is the physical world. The ego prefers us to be stuck in this world of problems and struggles. But our ego is nothing more than our idea of how to survive in the physical world. If it were truly a part of the physical world, we'd be able to check into a hospital for ego reconstruction, or even better, an "egoectomy." The ego is our idea of how to be safe and loved in our physical reality. We've separated from our Source when we engage exclusively with the illusions of the ego. It's only an idea and nothing more, yet this idea can keep us from knowing our Source. But with just the slightest alteration of this idea, we begin taming the ego.

All that we need to do is shift to the awareness that we can choose the ego when needed, *and* we can choose to select the power of our Source. Once we choose to tame the ego, we have the opportunity to make conscious contact in meditation and *know* God directly. We, then, are like the raindrop described by the 19th-century Urdu poet, Mirza Ghalib: "For the raindrop, joy is in entering the river . . . " An untamed ego will get in the way of this divine experience. In essence, this is entering an experience of oneness.

Oneness Is Indivisible

One quality that distinguishes our Source from the outer world is that it cannot be divided. Oneness defies being compartmentalized. For instance, our physical world is divided into dark and light, but the *source* of light, the sun, defies division. Or consider the nature of silence. It has been said that God's one and only voice is silence. No matter how you attempt to slice it up or cut it in half, silence is always silence. This indivisible root source of oneness is where the act of creation originates.

Indivisible oneness is the creative energy that turns a seed into a maple tree or a watermelon or a human being or anything else that's alive. It's invisible, omnipresent, and absolutely indivisible. We can't divide oneness. Meditation offers us the closest experience we can have of rejoining our Source and being in the oneness at the same time that we're embodied. This means that we have to tame our ego.

When we meditate, we begin to still the mind. As we get more and more adept at moving into inner silence, we come to know the peace of God in our entire being. We intuitively seek union with our generating Source. Silence, or meditation, is the path to that center. We can make conscious contact with God, transcend the limitations of a dichotomous world, and regain the power that is only available to us when we're connected to the Source. This is what I call *getting in the gap*. It's where we create, manifest, heal, live, and perform at a miraculous level. The gap is the powerful silence we can access through meditation. By entering the elusive gap between our thoughts, we can access the stillness that may have been unattainable in other meditation attempts.

Our Thoughts Keep Us from Silence

Our ultimate reason for meditating is to get in the gap where we enter the sacred space and know the unlimited power of our Source. Psalm 46:10 says: *"Be still, and know that I am God."* To know is to banish all doubt. Being still in meditation can take us to that awareness. But if you've tried meditating previously, what you're more likely to *know* is that your thoughts won't be still.

I find it helpful to think of my mind as a pond. The surface of the pond is similar to my mental chatter. On the surface of the pond are the disturbances. Here there are storms, debris, freezing and thawing, all on the surface. Beneath the pond surface, there is relative stillness. Here it is quiet and peaceful. If, as has been said, it's true that we have approximately 60,000 separate, often disconnected, thoughts during the day, then our mind is like a pond that's full of whitecaps from a choppy breeze. But beneath that surface chatter is the gap where we can know God and gain the unlimited power of reconnecting to our Source.

Meditating is a way of quieting our chatterbox thoughts and swimming below the surface. This is where we can be still and *know* (not *know about*) God. If we have approximately 60,000 thoughts every day, then in all of our waking hours, it's unlikely that we ever get to the point where there's any space between our thoughts. How could we? With one thought leading to the next, either rationally connected or otherwise, there's simply no time or place to get into the gap between our thoughts. Yet it's precisely in that gap that the magic and the infinite possibilities await us. I'll explain more about this euphoric gap and how to get there in the chapters that follow.

The practice of meditation takes us on a fabulous journey into the gap between our thoughts, where all the advantages of a peaceful, stress-free, healthier, fatigue-free life are available, but are simply side benefits. The paramount reason for doing this soul-nourishing meditation practice is to get in the gap between our thoughts and make conscious contact with the creative energy of life itself. But this is a choice that's entirely the responsibility of each individual. We have the potential to be instruments of the highest good for all concerned and to be miracle workers in our own lives. No person, government, or religion can legitimately claim to do this for us. In fact, I agree with Carl Jung, who once said that one of the main functions of formalized religion is to protect people against a direct experience of God.

I encourage you to master getting in the gap with the meditation called *Japa*, which I will describe in this book, and lead you through on the accompanying download. As you engage in prolonged meditation sessions, and experience what you bring back to the material world, you will know God . . . and you'll know why you choose to meditate.

"*Just as the pure crystal takes color from the object which is nearest to it, so the mind, when it is cleared of thought-waves, achieves sameness or identity with the object of its concentration.*"

— **Patanjali**

Chapter Two

The Gap and Why

Perhaps the most elusive space for human beings to enter is the gap between our thoughts. Usually we stay on one thought until another one takes over, leaving very little unused space. The spaces between our thoughts are brief, and seldom does anyone wonder what it would be like to have fewer thoughts, or what we'd find in the void between them. But the paradox is obvious. Thinking about what it would be like to be in the gap between our thoughts . . . is just another thought. Rather than expanding that space between, we move on to more thoughts. So why should we concern ourselves with entering the elusive gap? Because everything emerges from the void.

We get an inkling of why the gap between our thoughts is such a vital concept to grasp, and yes, to enter regularly, when we consider the following: *The place of "no thing" is where all that is "some thing" comes from.* We need the void of nothing in order to create something. As an example, consider any sound that you might make. Where does it come from? The void, the silence, the emptiness. Without the void, there would be noise all the time.

"It's the silence between the notes that makes the music" is an ancient Zen observation, which clarifies this idea. Imagine, if you can, music without pauses or silent spaces. Without the pauses for silence, the music would be one infinitely long note of noise. What we call music would be impossible. This is true for all of creation, including the world that you wish to create for yourself. Creativity itself is a function of the gap. The evidence for this is right in front of you.

For instance, when I look out the window, I see a tall palm tree that wasn't there ten years ago. Where did it come from? A seed. And where did the seed come from? An electron, or a subatomic quark. And where did the quark begin? The gap. The void. The silence. I observe a building that once was empty space. Its origin? In the mind of a human being. In the silence of a gap between contemplative, creative thoughts. I watch a little girl playing outside. What is her beginning? The seed, the egg. Yes, but ultimately it is the pure energy that is the creative force inside the tiniest of particles, from which all that is observable is capable of being observed.

St. Paul said, ". . . *that which is seen, hath not come from that which doth appear.*" No, indeed, it comes from the emptiness, the void, the space in between. In the silence between our thoughts, we find the possibilities of creative genius and spiritual awareness that elude us when we remain attentive only to our run-on thoughts.

The Gap and Our Busy Mind

Think of thoughts as things, which need silence between them to attract and manifest new forms into life. Two bricks can't be fastened together to form a wall without a space for mortar. The mortar itself is comprised of particles, which require spaces to allow them to become mortar. Our thoughts are the same. They require a pause between them to give life to what they represent separately. This is the gap, and it's a space that allows us to build, create, imagine, and manifest all that we're capable of creating with those thoughts. It's a place of ecstatic peace and serenity. It's a place that the ancient ones of the Far East called the *Tao,* and they were careful to elucidate that the Tao that can be described is not the Tao.

I can't describe the gap. Why? Because to do so is to leave the gap and revert to what is either in back of it or in front of it. I know the bliss I feel when I'm in the gap, but the moment I contemplate that bliss, I'm out of the gap. I think of the gap as God's house, since God is the omnipresent, invisible force that is in all of creation.

In every drop of human protoplasm, there's a "future-pull" that allows the physical journey to progress. The entire material-world journey is all in that microscopic drop of a seedling called our conception. It came from the *no-where,* shows up in *now-here,* and is heading back to *no-where.* It's all a question of spacing. There's something analogous with our thoughts as well. Within us is the almost unfathomable power to enter the gap between our thoughts, where we can commune silently with God and bring to life the same creativity that we see in the world of nature—of which we're an integral component.

That's right. We're just as much a part of the miraculously creative panorama of nature as the flowers, the sunsets, the seedlings turning into palm trees, the changing of the seasons, and everything else. It's being outside of the gap, and listening only to the ego, that keeps us from living at the level of being able to manifest.

The Gap and Manifesting

One of the most ego-free divine beings on this planet is a woman from India named Mother Meera. She has an ashram in Germany where she receives visitors from all over the world. As a child, she possessed exceptionally high spiritual qualities. By the age of three, she would report "going to various lights." This divine avatar attracts people from all over who come to receive her *darshan,* her silent bestowal of grace and light.

Through her grace and touch, Mother Meera is worshiped as a divine mother in India. I've spent time with her and have received her immaculate grace and touch. Mother Meera was instrumental in helping me formulate and write a book titled *Manifest Your Destiny: The Nine Spiritual Principles for Getting Everything You Want.* (You'll find a summary of these nine principles in a later chapter.) The nine principles emphasize that manifesting and attracting into our life all that we desire is based upon first becoming aware of our highest self and taming our ego. We also have to trust in the wisdom that created us, honor our worthiness to receive, embrace our own divinity, and meditate in order to make conscious contact with God.

Manifesting into life all that we desire through the principles I've elaborated in *Manifest Your Destiny* is a direct result of being able to enter the gap with ease and regularity. The gap, or space between our thoughts, is where all creation and manifestation originate. Another way of saying this comes from the words of Jesus from the gospel of John 6:63: *"The spirit gives life; the flesh profits nothing."*

To give life, we must enter the void, the silence between our thoughts. Here in the unbounded, the formless, the gap, is the source of all manifestation, all creation. This is the place where synchronicity begins to unfold and where the seemingly impossible takes place. Manifesting doesn't come from entering a religious building or subscribing to a particular organized faith. Mother Meera described this principle when asked if she wanted to begin a religion. Her response was, "No, the divine is the sea. All religions are rivers leading to the sea. Some rivers wind a great deal. Why not go to the sea directly?"

When Mother Meera held my head in her hands and gazed into my eyes, I felt God in her human form without the presence of an interfering ego. She showed me what it was like to let go of my own ego and enter the world of spirit, where the flesh actually means nothing. In a later chapter, I'll describe what Mother Meera and other divine souls of times gone by have taught me about staying in that blissful gap.

For now, why not heed the words of this blessed soul, who touched me and thousands of others, and *go to the sea directly*. Because we tend to stress limitations over potential, our culture doesn't readily encourage our potential for attracting anything we desire. So it may sound unbelievable that, by going within and entering the gap and simultaneously practicing ancient methods for staying there, we have greater potential than we realized.

We can negotiate the presence of what's missing by having the simple awareness of the silent, creative organizing force that allows everything to manifest. There's no place that God is not. If this God-force is everywhere, then it must be in you. And if it's everywhere, then it must be in all that you perceive to be missing from your life as well. So, manifesting is nothing more than a realignment of your inner intention in which you reconnect to that which is missing, via the God-force that you share with every one and every thing. And as strange as it may sound, this is accomplished by entering and staying in that gap between your thoughts, that silence between the notes. Mother Meera is correct: You *can* go to the sea directly. Let me help you now with a method for getting into that gap.

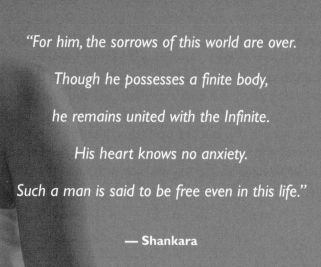

"For him, the sorrows of this world are over.

Though he possesses a finite body,

he remains united with the Infinite.

His heart knows no anxiety.

Such a man is said to be free even in this life."

— **Shankara**

Chapter Three

Getting in the Gap

Since silence is not really cultivated in our society, most people have a difficult time getting in the gap because they can't quiet their minds. I've developed my own technique for entering the gap and prolonging my visits there, which I'll guide you through on the audio download that accompanies this short book. In this chapter, I'll describe my technique, and in the following one, I'll write about *Japa,* which is a way to stay in the gap for more than just a few seconds at a time. To further assist you, you'll find a transcript of the guided meditations in the Appendix.

Read the following guidelines for some practical and valuable guidance before your first meditation. Then I'll introduce the meditation.

❋ *There's no such thing as a bad meditation.* Any time you spend in silence is valuable, even if your inner voice is persistent and loud. Don't judge it; just observe it. Simply observe yourself sitting there, and when a stray thought suddenly appears, just note it, and use its presence as a reminder to go back to the gap.

❋ *With time, your inner dialogue will shut down.* We all know that mastery is seldom achieved without practice. Meditation is no exception. Perhaps that's why it's called practice. With the passage of time, you'll easily slip into the gap with joyous anticipation of reuniting with God.

❋ *There's no right or wrong time to meditate.* Each of us finds our most comfortable time of day, so don't try to do this on someone else's schedule. You can slip into the gap frequently if you take advantage of a two-minute stop at a traffic light, a pause in a meeting, a trip to the rest room, or the time you spend waiting for an appointment.

❋ *There's no correct meditation length.* I find that approximately 20 minutes per session twice daily is optimal for me. However, even a few moments can be nurturing. I've also learned that a two- or three-hour flight is a grand opportunity for me to spend an extended period of time in the gap, and that the time passes in what seems like a few moments.

❋ *There's no correct posture or place for meditating.* Find what makes you comfortable and trust it. Sitting, lying down, kneeling—whatever works for you is the perfect posture. Anyplace at all can serve as your location. Since I travel so much, I'm not particular about location, while some people I know use the same posture, the same chair, and the same time every day. Whatever "floats your boat," as my teenagers say, is fine.

Now that we've dispensed with most of the have-to's and have rid ourselves of any rigidity connected to our time in the gap, let's go there!

My Favorite Method for Entering the Gap

As I've already described, we tend to have a thought, and then a second thought, without noticing any space between them. Remember that the gap is the space between our thoughts. It's the void from which all creation emerges— "God's house" is a metaphor I like. The first thing we need to do is find a way to simply observe what it feels like to be in this gap. We can begin to get that feeling by using the first ten words of The Lord's Prayer: *"Our Father Who art in heaven, hallowed be Thy name."* Instead of thinking of this as a religious exercise, think of it as a method for entering the domain of Spirit.

In a quiet space, in whatever posture is most comfortable for you, close your eyes, and put all of your attention on the word *Our*. See it appear on the inner screen of your mind. Repeat the sound to yourself several times, "Our,

Our, Our." Focus all of your energy on this word. Now shift your inner attention to the word *Father*. See it appear in your mind, and think only of this word. Repeat it over and over.

Now comes the indescribably exquisite part, which each of us experiences in our own way. Make a quick adjustment in your mind, and follow this with an ever-so-slight movement of your head toward the left. Put all of your attention in the space in your mind between the words *Our* and *Father*. Stay in this space between these two words for 10 or 15 seconds, and note how it feels to rest your mind on nothing but that space. Picture the gap, and experience the peaceful and nurturing quality of being in it. You have now initiated the process of entering the gap.

(In the next chapter, I describe the ancient and powerful technique for staying in the gap for extended periods of your meditation time.)

Due to your mind's habit of focusing on a thought, rather than the gap *between* your thoughts, you'll undoubtedly find a thought creeping in. If you get out of the gap for a few seconds, immediately but gently pull your inner attention back to the first word, *Our,* then to *Father,* and ever so slightly move your head to the left and reenter the gap. You'll find it slightly easier to do the second time. From then on, use any thought as a clue to go forward, and repeat the technique. So, at the next thought, move from the gap to the right (we arrange words from left to right in our writing so right is forward and left is backwards) and focus your attention on *Father.* Then move forward to the word *Who,* and hold your attention here. Then go back (to the left) in your mind to the space between these two words. When you've experienced the gap, go to the word *Who,* and then to the word *art.* After a few seconds, go back to the gap between them. Repeat this gap exercise until you've meditated through the first ten words.

Everyone I've led through this particular gap exercise has exclaimed in one way or another that it was the first time they were able to silence their mind. More than anything else, they report that the gap experience provided them with feelings of serenity and calmness. It's in this quiet, unbounded gap that the solutions to all of our problems as well as the ability to manifest and create are found. This joyful experience is our conscious contact with the peace of God. It's what I think the world's leading 17th-century scientist, Blaise Pascal, had in mind when he observed: "All man's miseries derive from not being able to sit quietly in a room alone."

Now, let's move on to a powerful tool for staying in the gap and bringing to daily life much that you previously thought was beyond your capabilities.

"With eyes brimming with love, sing his name.

All inner mysteries will be disclosed. . . .

O dear one, keep chanting God's name while sitting,

or standing, or involved in the world."

— **Swami Muktananda**

Chapter Four

Staying in the Gap with Japa

Many years ago, I learned a meditation technique that was taught by a great teacher in India. The meditation is known as Japa, and it has been around for many centuries. Essentially, *Japa* means "to say the name of God repeatedly." Mother Meera, whom I wrote about earlier, includes Japa in her teachings. She has written, "I suggest that you do your job and your duties wholeheartedly and joyfully, and bring peace and happiness in your family and in your surroundings; do Japa, the chanting or repeating of the name of God, and ask for whatever you want, and you shall receive it."

I know, from my own experience, that many people who haven't tried Japa are apt to scoff at this idea. If you count yourself as one of those individuals, I sincerely encourage you to open your mind to this form of wisdom, which has been practiced for thousands of years by our most enlightened ancestors.

Consider the following: In the opening words of John I:I: "*In the beginning was the Word, and the Word was with God, and the Word was God.*"

This is strikingly similar to a verse from the Rig Veda: "*In the beginning was Brahman, with whom was the Word; and the Word was truly the supreme Brahman.*"

Also, in Proverbs: "*The name of the Lord is a strong tower: the righteous run into it and are safe.*"

The Hindu Scriptures say: "*Take refuge in his name.*"

The *Yoga Aphorisms of Patanjali* bring Japa into the meditative state with these words: "But now, if we introduce into this reverie the repetition of the name of God, we shall find that we can control our moods, despite the interference of the outside world . . . the name of God will change the climate of your mind. It cannot do otherwise. . . . We cannot long continue to repeat any word without beginning to think about the reality which it represents."

The sound *ah* within the name *God* is the same sound around the world. We find *ah* in Allah, Krishna, Jehovah, and Ra, for a few examples. When repeated as a mantra while in the gap, this sound keeps us in a prolonged state of conscious contact with our Source. It also introduces us to the highest consciousness level, where we realign our inner intention to the creative force that we're a part of. Essentially, I was taught that the expression of the word or sound that means *God* brings us into contact with God. God is the basic fact of the universe, symbolized with this most natural and comprehensive of all sounds. It's no accident that the words *omnipotent, omniscience,* and *omnipresent* contain the sound of God.

In addition to being the same sound that's in the name for God in almost all languages, *ah* is also the only sound that we can make that requires virtually no effort. The effortless perfection of God is expressed when the teeth, tongue, lips, and jaw all remain stationary, not touching each other. The only sound we can make then is *ah,* or God. As Patanjali put it in his *Yoga Sutra:*

> *The word, which expresses Him, is aum*
> *This word must be repeated with meditation upon its meaning.*
> *Hence comes knowledge of the Atman and destruction of*
> *the obstacles to that knowledge.*

If you think that this is a radical idea, remember that Japa has been practiced in enlightened circles for thousands of years. Japa meditation is a way of moving into the highest levels of awareness where we know that "in the beginning was the Word . . . and the Word was God." This means *all* beginnings, including the process of manifestation, which is the beginning of creation out of the void (or the gap), into the manifest world of form.

Japa and Manifesting

There's a spiritual energy that connects every thing and every one in the universe. This is the one power that is called by many names, all of which contain the creation sound of *ah*. When we practice the repetition of this sound and focus on its meaning, it leads us to inner realignments where we begin the process of attracting into our life what appeared to be missing . . . but which we were spiritually connected to all along. As Patanjali puts it, "Mere repetition of God's name is, of course insufficient. . . . We must meditate upon its meaning. But the process follows naturally upon the other. If we persevere in our repetition, it will lead us inevitably into meditation."

In meditation, while repeating the sound of God, we can place our intention on what we would like to attract and use this sound as an attractor for manifesting. In practice, we actually become the universal sound itself. This is the *yoga,* or the coming together, of the observer and the observed. We're participating in the act of creation and manifesting, and will begin to experience an overwhelming sense of bliss and peace while practicing this Japa exercise. I encourage you to make this sound of creation your mantra for the time that you're in the gap.

This is how you do Japa:

Begin with The Lord's Prayer exercise in the previous chapter. When you're in the sacred silence of the space between the words of The Lord's Prayer, begin the repetition of *ah,* the sound of creation. First gently note the feeling of being at one with God. Then attend totally to the sound of God and what you desire in your life. This mantra, when repeated silently within the gap, becomes the attractor energy pattern for manifesting into your life-space the God-force of spiritual energy that is omnipresent in our universe—and to which you're already connected. (The nine principles I described in *Manifest Your Destiny* help in this process. They're summarized at the end of this chapter for your reference.)

Imagine that you'd like to attract more abundance into your life. While in the gap, first focus on the feeling of being connected to God. When you do so, you're embracing your own divinity. Then place your inner attention on seeing abundance coming into your world. Let go of *how,* and simply say *yes.* Detach from the outcome, and repeat the sound of God (*ah*), knowing that abundance will manifest in the form of the highest good for all concerned in your world. Use this Japa meditation to make conscious contact with your spiritual energy, rather than treating it like an ego trick in which you seek special favors. You're letting go, letting God, and knowing that you're united with this creative force. Detaching from the how and when keeps you focused on your spiritual connection. The abundance will show up—simply know it.

Staying in the gap is accomplished through Japa, and it has a threefold purpose. First, we begin to experience the benefits of less stress, more peace, less fatigue, more energy—and we look and feel younger and happier. Second, we move into a creative place while in the gap where we can use Japa to attract anything into our life that we choose. Third, and most significant, we make conscious contact with God the source of the energy, which makes peace, joy, higher energy, and everything that shows up possible.

As Patanjali put it, "The physical strength gained in a gymnasium can be used later for practical purposes. The mental strength gained through these exercises in concentration can be used for the most practical purpose of all; to unite ourselves with the Atman."

Here is a summary of the nine spiritual principles from *Manifest Your Destiny*:

1. *Become aware of your highest self.* This awareness helps you know that you are more than merely a physical creation.

2. *Trust yourself so that you trust the wisdom that created you.* This principle establishes you as one and the same with the universal God-force.

3. *Realize that you are more than an organism in an environment.* You are an environorganism. This principle establishes that there is no separation between you and anything outside you in the material world.

4. *Know that you can attract to yourself what you desire.* This principle establishes your power to attract that which you are already connected to.

5. *Honor your worthiness to receive.* This principle affirms that you are worthy of all that is attracted to your life.

6. *Connect to the divine Source with unconditional love.* This principle creates an awareness of the significance of accepting your manifestations with absolute love.

7. *Meditate to the sound of creation.* This principle gives you the tools for vibrating to the sounds that are in the world of creation.

8. *Patiently detach from the outcome.* This principle emphasizes the need to remove demands and become infinitely patient.

9. *Receive your manifestations with gratitude and generosity.* This principle teaches you the value of taming the ego while being thankful and serving others with your manifestations.

**Q: Why should one offer everything
to the divine?**

A: *Offering everything, pure and impure, is the best
and quickest way to develop spiritually. If you offer
everything to the Divine, the Divine will accept and
change it, even the worst things. It is not what you
offer but that you offer which is important. Offer
everything, and you will acquire the habit of thinking
always about God. That will change you.*

— **Mother Meera**

FAQs Regarding the Gap and Japa Meditation

Over the years since the publication of *Manifest Your Destiny* and the guided meditation CD *Meditations for Manifesting*, I've received many letters and queries concerning the entire process of getting into the gap and using Japa for manifesting. Here are some of the most frequently asked questions (FAQs), with my responses:

Q. I'm too busy to take time every day for meditation. How can I fit it into my schedule?

A: I give the same answer that I do when people complain about not having enough time for exercise. I personally don't have the time to be sick, so I take the time to be healthy. You must make time, either by waking up 20 minutes earlier, or going to sleep 20 minutes later. Also, many moments during the day are opportunities to meditate. Even a few minutes at a traffic light ten times a day is better than nothing.

The fact is, once you become accustomed to regular meditation, you'll enjoy the discipline so much that you'll find yourself making it a top priority in your life. You'll feel so great after meditation that you won't want to deny yourself this reward. Make a 30-day commitment to Japa and getting inside the gap, and you will have developed a new habit. It's a habit that will serve you well for the rest of your life.

Q. *I can't seem to quiet my mind and shut down my inner dialogue. Why do these thoughts keep occupying my mind when I try to meditate?*

A. You're doing in meditation what you've been conditioned to do with your mind for an entire lifetime. Aimless thinking of disconnected thoughts is how you've trained your mind to behave. You're going into a retraining mode when you practice meditation regularly. If you suddenly had to use only your left hand after a lifetime of right-handedness, it would at first be awkward and darn near impossible. But eventually, with perseverance and practice, you'd succeed as a lefty.

The mantra of *ah,* along with the exercise of The Lord's Prayer to enter the gap, is designed to help you retrain your mind. When you notice a thought invading your quiet space, be aware of it, and use it as a reminder to return to the mantra. Keep your attention on the concept of being in conscious contact with God, and the essence of what you intend to manifest. With practice, you'll find that transcending your haphazard thoughts is just as natural as eating with your right hand.

Q. Whenever I try to meditate, I end up falling asleep. What should I do to avoid this?

A. This is only a temporary condition. Sleeping is a way of avoiding the discipline of meditation. Don't judge it. Allow yourself to drift off to sleep if that's what your body demands. You're not doing anything wrong by sleeping. You *will* come out of that sleep. When you do, note it, and then return to the gap and Japa. If you refuse to judge it or to see yourself as a failure, you'll see sleep for what it is: a need to rest. Eventually that pattern will cease. Often it's difficult to make a distinction between sleep and deep meditation in the gap. Both are experiences of non-thought that provide you with a sense of restful peace and tranquility. By staying with the Japa mantra, you'll soon wish to avoid sleep, since it will take you away from the ecstasy of soul nourishment that Japa provides. Meanwhile, sleep if you're inclined . . . until you're no longer so inclined.

Q. *During the manifesting process, can I place my attention on more than one thing that I'd like to attract into my life?*

A. My children and I play a game in the swimming pool called **tegwar** (**t**he **e**xciting **g**ame **w**ithout **a**ny **r**ules). The object is to hit the side of the pool with a volleyball, behind a defender. Every time an argument ensues about whether I'm allowed to swim underwater, or pull them out of their goal, or get out of the pool and charge them from behind, I always take the point and say, "Tegwar."

Japa meditation is like tegwar. You can do whatever you want and it will work for you. Yes, you can place your attention on healing your sore back, and in the next breath focus on selling your home or having a more loving relationship with one of your children. I've found that staying focused on the connection with the divine allows my thoughts to diminish and my inner attention to concentrate on the feeling of love and peace. I've stopped manifesting more "stuff" into my life, and instead, my intentions are all about serving; and staying in a peaceful, loving place. However, when I did practice

Japa to attract something I desired into my life, it always seemed to show up, but seldom in the form or on the schedule I had laid out in my mind.

The key to Japa and manifesting is repeating the sound of *ah*. You need to feel the energy so strongly that you're literally negotiating the presence of what you desire by being at one with the same force that you perceive to be missing. There are no rules or limits to what you can attract.

Q. I've been doing Japa for some time, and I have yet to see the object of my desire arrive into my life. Why?

A. This is a question you'll learn to avoid asking—ever! In *A Course in Miracles,* there's an observation that gives you the answer: "Infinite patience produces immediate results." It means that when you're infinitely patient, you have an inner knowing that you and God are connected, and therefore nothing is truly missing. Whatever it is that you seek, the essence of it is for you to be at peace. The immediate result you receive from infinite patience is peace. You know that all is in divine order. Your desire to attract anything is an energy. That energy is always for the best. In the end, everything will be great. If it's not great, then it's not the end.

I've seen the power of Japa at work in many ways in my life. There have been many difficult situations I've been faced with that appeared to be the exact opposite of my manifestation efforts. Yet I've come to trust that it's always for the best. What once seemed calamitous now is seen as a divine blessing. Once again, your job is not to say *how* or *when,* but to say *yes.* After *yes,* become the observer and give thanks for everything. Every time I pick up a coin on the street, I view it as a symbol of the abundance that God sends into my life, and I feel gratitude. I always say, "Thank You, God, for everything." Never do I ask, "Why only a penny?"

Q. How do I know when I'm in conscious contact with God? Could it just be my ego taking over?

A. You're always being encouraged to see the kingdom of heaven within and to embrace your own divinity, yet it's still difficult to overcome conditioned beliefs that God is separate. You've been raised on separateness, and you're sold on the concept.

"God is love and he that dwelleth in Love dwelleth in God" (I John 4:16). *"On that day, you will know that I am in our Father, and you in me, and I in you"* (I John 14:20).

There's no separation when you're in a state of love or peace, which is your connection, period. When you doubt your connection, you're living by your ego, and manifesting is impossible. Remember again, it's the spirit that gives life. The flesh counts for nothing!

Q. *Can I really participate in manifesting? Isn't this a quality that's reserved for highly evolved spiritual masters?*

A. You are a uniquely divine creation. You share the same life force that was in Moses, Jesus, Buddha, Mother Teresa, Mohammed, St. Francis, or any divine being you can name. There is only one life force, one divine power. When it manifests as doubt, fear, hate, or even evil, it's still the one power moving away from God in ego consciousness. When it manifests as faith, joy, forgiveness, hope, light, and love, it's the same force—either moving toward God or in harmony with God consciousness. *"Truly, I say to you, he who believes in me, the works that I do, he will do also; and greater works than these shall he do; because I am going to the father"* (John 14:12). Keep in mind that you can't move to higher ground if you're clutching on to a lower level, refusing to let go. You can't enter the manifesting world of Spirit if you refuse to let go of your physical-world attachment. Yes, you are divine. Yes, you can do all that any spiritual master has accomplished and even more. Know it.

Q. Can I manifest into my life even if I feel that I don't deserve more?

A. It's very unlikely. You must learn to honor your worthiness to receive. The nature of the universe is abundance. The Scriptures say, *"All that I have is thine."* Think of the ocean as the Source. You can take as much as you desire from the ocean and it never impacts the amount available. It's infinite in supply. You're entitled to as much as you desire. An eyedropper once a year or a million gallons a day—it makes no difference to the ocean.

If you feel unworthy of what you'd like to manifest, that's the attractor energy pattern that you'll connect to, and you'll ultimately act upon the thought, *I don't deserve what I'd like.* The universe will then respond in kind, and even if what you desired showed up and knocked at your door, you'd still act as if it didn't belong to you, or you wouldn't believe it was for you in the first place. You're entitled to the unlimited abundance of this world. Know it, and you activate the force to attract it into your life.

Q. *Should I share what I'd like to accomplish or attract with those closest to me?*

A. A definitive *no way!* This is the surest way to invite ego into your meditation practice. This entire business of Japa and the gap is between you and God. The moment you try explaining it to others, you're in the position of defending yourself. This will bring your manifestation process to a halt. Why? Because it's the spirit that gives life—not the flesh.

Quantum physics states that particles themselves do not create more particles. What is needed is that invisible energy, the source of all life. Do all that you can to keep your ego out of your meditation practice. Share it with God. Period!

These are some of the most frequently asked questions, with my candid responses. In the next chapter, you'll find letters I've received from people who have put this Japa experience of meditation into their lives.

Dear Wayne,

The purpose of this meditation is to end

the sufferings of human beings through the

manifestation of their desires. Before I developed

and offered the technique, I prayed with Siva and

Nandi that I would never allow it to be misused.

That is the reason why I chose you.

— Sri Guruji

Chapter Six

Testimonials about Japa Meditation

Over the years, I've received a lot of heartfelt correspondence describing the unique ways in which people have manifested through meditation. I've selected the following letters for you to read, and I invite you to contact me about your own experiences with this meditation technique (you can write to me in care of Hay House, via their P.O. Box address).

Jean wrote to me after a friend who was working on some meditation issues asked her to listen to my tapes:

I listened to the tapes and was so impressed with them that I couldn't get them out of my mind—especially the concepts on manifesting. I began that day to apply the principles you shared in this tape presentation. I found them working in such an unbelievable manner. I've used them now for several months, and everything that I've sought to manifest has come into my life. It's like I've tasted a delicious fruit and find that I can't get my appetite for the fruit satisfied.

The card I received from Sharon was a work of art in and of itself. Her note was written inside one of her hand-painted original collages. In it, she described finding outlets for her artwork:

I began doing your Meditations for Manifesting *tape morning and night a little over two months ago. When I started, there were no locations for selling my artwork (no where!). I now have several museums and galleries carrying my work (now here!). Amazing stuff, this meditation!*

৵৵৵৵৵৵

After attending a presentation I gave in Phoenix, Cindie began talking to and meditating on her problem:

I attended your June presentation in Phoenix and appreciated the information you provided. I was scheduled to have surgery on my sinuses in August. I'd had this same painful surgery four years ago and was recently devastated to learn that I needed to have polyps removed from my sinuses again. After hearing your presentation, I immediately started talking to the polyps, asking them to leave and letting them know that their purpose inside my sinuses was over. I also began doing the ah *meditation every morning, and the meditation at night focusing on healthy sinuses.*

Last week the doctor let me know that my sinuses were free of polyps and that surgery wasn't required!

I love reading about the way meditation works for different people. This letter from Denise is one of my favorites:

> *Just a quick note to say thank you for coming to San Diego in February. My mom flew out from Iowa just to see you that Sunday. She has always admired and respected you, and to see and hear you was the highlight of her trip.*
>
> *We both meditated to the meditation CD that week, and the very first day I was listening to the CD, I couldn't help but love the wind chimes on the tape, and I said in my meditation that I needed wind chimes.*
>
> *That afternoon, a friend of mine who never stops by came by unannounced. She was dropping off a belated birthday present. She has given me a gift certificate every year for the past five years. This time I opened the package . . . and yes, you know what was in it . . . wind chimes! That was like a level three in manifesting!*

Sheryl told me how she began to look at everything with unconditional love, and how she eliminated stress in more ways than one:

> *I'd been experiencing a lot of stress in my life, and I don't feel that way now that I've started to meditate. When I feel the stress coming on, I'll meditate alone in my office, or silently. I've also caught myself doing this when someone in my office is on the "attack" mode.*
>
> *Wonderful things happened to me on the first day of meditating. I received a $10,000 bonus check, a $10 refund from an emergency clinic, and a message from my daughter's orthodontist saying that her braces could come off six months earlier than scheduled! In my morning meditation, I had meditated on peace and security.*
>
> *The gratitude meditation that I did later that day was certainly as heartfelt as it could be.*

Dave wrote to tell me that he and his wife, Gail, were experiencing miracles as a result of their meditation:

>   *I want to thank you again for all of your help. The ah meditations have created miracles for me: a new home (my wife, Gail's, dream house), a job that I can finally feel successful at, and excellent health after two bouts with cancer—I just got a clean bill of health this past Monday.*
>
>   *I've learned that taking complete and total responsibility for my own life has allowed me to make the changes necessary to achieve success, peace, and happiness.*

First-time author Mariann sent me a wonderful letter in which she said that she completed a book proposal and five chapters after only one week of daily meditating:

>   *I sent the proposal to two publishers and two literary agents. A week later, I heard back from an editor. He called me at 8:30 in the morning to tell me how*

much he loved the book and told me that he would have a definite answer for me within four weeks. The following week, I got a call from a literary agent in San Francisco who wants to represent me. Wow!

My husband is walking around in a stupor, saying, "Do you realize that it's been only six weeks since you said 'I'm going to write a book'—and now it's half-written and you already have an agent and a publisher? Let me listen to those tapes!"

ঙঞ্জ ঙঞ্জ ঙঞ্জ

I receive a lot of letters from Australia, where I speak frequently. This one from Sandy is representative of the life changes that can occur as a result of meditation:

Two years ago, I was running a surfwear company here on the Sunshine Coast that I had started so I could be my own boss—not realizing that it would mean I'd end up having no time for myself or my children because I'd be doing nothing but working. That business got me into so much debt (more than $100,000), and I was receiving the Sole Parents Pension just to help me survive financially. My stress levels were through the roof, and I was financially, mentally, emotionally, and spiritually a mess—then I began to have physical challenges. That's when I knew it was time to stop (don't ask me why I waited that long!), but I had no idea what else I could possibly do.

I had no real skills or expertise in any area, and all I really wanted was to be able to spend time looking after myself while watching my children grow, but I dreamed of something that would help me experience abundance and prosperity in all areas of my life.

I'd written a list a few months before of my "ideal day." It had things like meditate, exercise, swim in my pool, study personal growth by listening to inspiring tapes and reading books, help others to achieve everything they can, learn to public-speak, and spend time outdoors. After reading through my list, I said to a friend, "If I do all these things in a day—I'll never have the time to work."

Personal development had been a real passion of mine for the previous seven years, and I really wanted to see you when you were touring, but simply couldn't justify spending the money on a ticket when I had so many other debts. I was extremely fortunate to be chosen to staff the event, and was very grateful that I got to watch almost the entire seminar. When you spoke about your new CD, Meditations for Manifesting, *I rushed out to get it at the break, but you had already sold out. That's okay—patience was one thing I really needed to learn!*

Within a few days, I'd managed to buy one, and immediately began using it morning and night. I followed your instructions to the letter.

I look back even now, and cannot believe how quickly opportunities magically appeared in my life. Within weeks, I stumbled across an ad for an international personal-development company that was looking for self-motivated people with a strong work ethic. That's me! Roughly 18 months later, my life reads straight off my "ideal day" list.

I now work from home and have an international business marketing self-empowerment courses and seminars. I only work when I want to, so I get to enjoy my two beautiful children and the Sunshine Coast where we live. I have the time to swim and walk along the beach every day. I earn a six-figure income working part-time (that in itself is a miracle!). I've been able to take my children to Bali for the school holidays and recently spent a month in Hawaii learning, relaxing, and swimming with the dolphins. I get to talk with people on a daily basis, helping them achieve their dreams. I've even had the opportunity to speak in front of hundreds of people to inspire and motivate them to transform their lives. My business is the personal-development industry, so as part of that, I meditate, and read and listen to tapes daily. It's now my work!

All I can say is WOW. I manifested a miracle into my life. I've achieved a wonderful balance in my body, mind, and spirit, and have experienced financial abundance as well.

Two years ago, I was on the Sole Parents Pension, alternating between crying and feeling so sorry for myself, and screaming like a madwoman at my children, feeling as though I had no control over any aspect of my life. And that all changed in a heartbeat.

Now I'm living a lifestyle I once only dreamed of. I understand that I'm the co-creator of my life and feel grateful and blessed that I've made that discovery, and I want to thank you so much for your wonderful CD that helped change the direction of my life.

One of the reasons I'm so fond of the following letter from Janet in Illinois is that she has a healthy regard for one of nine principles I've written about: her worthiness to receive:

I'm writing to tell you the story of how I've manifested my destiny. I read your book, Manifest Your Destiny, *and heard you speak at the Whole Life Expo in Chicago a couple of years ago. Even though I had read all of your previous books and listened to your* tapes, I had never practiced meditation, nor had I really developed a personal spiritual life. You suggested the possibility of being able to attract the kind of life most desired, and even though I was honestly very skeptical, I decided that it was worth a try. Here's my story:

I am a graphic designer, married with four kids, not an unhappy person. I've hated every job I've ever held except one—teaching graphic design part-time at a community college. That night I heard you speak, I was feeling especially restless and dissatisfied with many things, mostly my job. I decided to try your sound meditation, bought the CD, and went home to begin. What a turning point in my life.

It was difficult at first—nothing really happened during meditation—but gradually I began to notice a new peacefulness settling into my mental life. I meditated about what kind of life I wanted to manifest. It became extremely clear to me over a period of a few weeks that only one job had ever been satisfying—that's the one I should try to manifest. Even though I had taught part-time off and on for a number of years,

I couldn't teach full-time for a variety of reasons—
mainly, no positions were open, and I didn't have a
master's degree.

But I felt so strongly that the sound meditation was
changing things in my life that I set out to create a
position for myself in the community college graphic
design department. Within two weeks, I had an amazing
phone call from the college. One of the full-time teachers
was having a difficult pregnancy and was going to have
to stay home for many months—could I possibly substitute for her? I trusted the Universe, quit my other
job, and said yes. It turned out that she was gone for
two full semesters with health problems, and I was
allowed to teach full-time for the whole year. I loved it!
During this time, I continued to meditate and to build
my personal spiritual relationship with the Universe.

When she came back, I was demoted to an occa-
sional part-time teacher again. But I had grown strong
in my trust of the Universe by this time and set out to
create the full-time position I wanted so much. It's a
long story of incredible obstacles. By this time I had

two daughters in college, which required a large cash flow. The master's degree I needed was only offered at the University of Illinois, 100 miles from my home, no part-time or outreach classes; only full-time on-campus students are accepted. I had no extra money, no job, no extra time to take off for college at age 50, etc., etc.

Then the miracles began happening again. I started a little graphic design business from my home. Immediately I had lots of clients. A printer made a "mistake" and sent me a commission check for printing a job for one of my clients. When I called to discuss the "mistake," he realized how much business I was sending him and decided to put me on the payroll. I would do no extra work, just send him my print jobs, and he would pay me 10 percent of every print bill.

Now my income just went up—a lot—and I was doing no more work, spending no more time. I applied and was accepted at the university. Through much lobbying, I worked out an acceptable plan for commuting 100 miles each way two or three days a week for four semesters, living on campus only one semester.

To make a long story as short as possible, the universe opened a path for me. Step by step, I watched as obstacles fell away. The big snowstorms always hit on days when I wasn't making the drive to Champaign; money magically flowed into my life just when I needed it; freelance job deadlines missed school project deadlines in a rhythmic flow.

Now, don't misunderstand—this wasn't easy. I worked my butt off, rarely slept more than five hours a night, commuted, did freelance, studied, taught part-time, and fulfilled family obligations—all with no guarantee of any kind that a position would become available for me at the college.

Then, guess what? One of the full-time professors decided to retire at the end of the spring semester when I was to graduate. What a coincidence! I applied for the position along with lots of other people, many who were very qualified, and all who were younger. By this time I was 52. And you guessed the end of my story—this week I got the call offering me a full-time teaching position in the college graphic design department.

My story probably doesn't have all the drama of some of the stories you've been told, but for me it's a real-life miracle. I haven't told this story to other people, but I wanted to write and tell you.

Janet's story is one that most of us can relate to because it does indeed have drama—it features the drama of an individual life, which each one of us is responsible for. No one else can do it for you. Only you can manifest your real-life miracles.

Appendix

"*Getting in the Gap*" Audio Download Transcript

*[**Editor's Note:** We have included the text of the meditations
here in case you'd like to follow along or would like to
refer back to it at a future date.]*

I t has been said that it's the space between the bars that
holds the tiger. And it's the silence between the notes that
makes the music. It is out of the silence, or "the gap," or
that space between our thoughts, that everything is created—including our own bliss. The reason for wanting to get
into the gap is not so much to give you a sense of peace,
which you will, of course, receive, and it's not so much to
make you feel rested, as it will—you can get the equivalent
of a night's sleep by spending a few moments in the gap. And

it's not even to make you feel younger, which of course it will do. The purpose of entering the gap, the space between your thoughts, on a regular basis, is to be able to make conscious contact with God.

By making conscious contact with God, it is said that you will come to know the power of that Source and use that power to attract anything into your life. God is that one force in the universe that is indivisible. There's only one force, one power, and you can't divide it. And the only experience that you can have in your physical world, which is indivisible, is also that of silence, or "in the gap." Everything else can be divided: up/down; right/wrong; good/bad; male/female; even life/death. But silence, no matter how many times you cut it in half, you still have the same. In the gap, you are making conscious contact with the indivisible force that is the source of all of your power and all of your joy and all of your fulfillment in your life. The gap is the space between your thoughts.

The reason that it is so difficult for so many people to enter this gap is because we have so many thoughts going on all day long. It is said that the average person has 60,000 thoughts every single day. The problem is that we have the same 60,000 thoughts each day. Our mind is very noisy. And very seldom in a place of silence. If you could reduce the number of thoughts that you have from 60,000 to 20,000, there would be more gaps. If you could reduce it down to 6,000, there'd be far more gaps. And if you could reduce it to a few hundred, of course there'd be many, many gaps.

What we're looking for here is a time each day that you can reduce the amount of thoughts that you're having so that the gaps will expand and you can enter them. It is said that it is very difficult to enter this gap, or to make conscious contact with God, because we are so busy in our minds, being concerned with our own ego and all of the things that separate us from our Source, from God. What I've done here on this CD is offered you an opportunity, a way to slip into the gap, on a regular basis, that is quite simple; and while you're in that gap, I'm going to offer you the *opportunity* to practice something that has been taught over the centuries, as far back as 2,500 years ago, called *Japa*.

Japa is the repetition, or the sound, of the name of God. It is the sound that is in the name for God in virtually all languages and all cultures. Whether it's Allah or Krishna or God or Adonai or Yaweh or Ra or Kali Durga—on and on, the names go, but inside each one of those names is a sound. It's the magical sound. If you look at the New Testament and open up the book of John, you will see the opening words say: *"In the beginning was the Word, and the Word was with God, and the Word was God."*

I was taught by a great teacher at one time that whenever you're having a problem, whenever you're struggling with anything in your life, whenever your mind is filled with the struggles of your life, the way to make that problem go away, in that instant, is to think of God, rather than the problem that you're focused on. In this CD, I'm asking you not only to think of God, but to repeat the sound of God while you are in the gap, or the space between your thoughts. And while you are there, if you repeat this sound, the sound of *ah,* on a regular basis each day, you will find your meditation not only nurturing your soul, but you'll find yourself able to manifest and attract into your life virtually anything that you place your attention upon. You no longer have to think of it as a difficult thing to enter into this gap. The space *between* your thoughts can be entered and regularly visited with the practice of Japa while you're there by following the guidelines.

What I'm offering here on this CD is two versions of this technique for moving into the gap. I suggest that you try the first ten-or-so-minute version, which will allow you to get the experience of what it means to be in the gap. And then following that, on the next track, there is a longer version, a 20-minute version, in which you can spend much more time in the gap. You'll find that once you've begun doing this on a regular basis, you'll want to spend less time on the words, and more of that precious, beautiful time in the gap, where you're making conscious contact with God.

I developed this technique for entering into the gap because I had, at one time, found it difficult myself to get into that quiet space between my thoughts, where all creation takes place, where I make conscious contact with God, or with my Source. What I'm asking you to do is think of a ten-word passage from the most well-known prayer in Western civilization. It's called "The Lord's Prayer." What I'd like to do is offer the first ten words of this prayer, and in each one of these words, I'd like you to practice moving into the gap, as you see these words coming onto the screen of your inner mind. While you are in the gap, I will ask you to *practice repeating* the sound of the name of God, or the sound of *ah* as a mantra to keep you connected to your Source, and away from the thoughts that will penetrate your mind, which is really your ego at work, trying to convince you that this isn't going to work. But it will. Entering into the gap is a mental image that you can practice. Let's begin.

Track 1

What I would like you to do first is get comfortable, close your eyes, be in any position that appeals to you—whether it's lying down or sitting up, or in a yoga position, or on your favorite chair—and put your hands very lightly on your lap, face up, with your forefinger and your thumb *just barely* touching each other so that you can make an imaginary circuit between the words that you are hearing, the sound that you are hearing here, and your heart.

I'm going to ask you now to put all of your attention on the word *Our,* O-u-r. Place your attention on the word *Our,* and see it appearing on the screen of your mind. **[Pause]** Now I would like you to move your attention off of the word *Our* and onto the word *Father.* See the word *Father* appearing before you. Now what I'd like you to do is slip back into the space between those two words in your mind. Go back now to the space between *Our* and *Father.* And just rest there. Now I would like you to repeat that sound of God, the sound of *ah,* Japa. While in the gap: "Ahh-hhhhhhhh. Ahhhhhhhhhh." If any thought enters your mind, return to the sound of *ah.* Staying in the gap between *Our* and *Father.*

Now move your attention to the word *Father* again and see *Father* appearing on the screen of your inner mind. **[Pause]** Now move forward in your mind to the word *Who,* and see the word *Who* appearing on the screen of your mind. Now instantly slip back into the gap between the words *Father* and *Who,* and put all of your attention just on this gap and nothing more. **[Pause]** And now we will do Japa: "Ahhhhhhhhhh. Ahhhhhhhhhh."

Now, on the inner screen of your mind, see the word *Who* flash before you. W-h-o. Put all of your attention on the word *Who*. Now shift forward to the word *art*. Put all of your attention on the word *art.* Now instantly shift backwards into the space between *Who* and *art,* and stay in that space, with no thoughts penetrating. **[Pause]** *Feel* the lightness of the gap. **[Pause]** And now Japa: "Ahhhhhhhhhh. Ahhhhh-hhhhh."

Now shift the inner screen of your mind to the word *art.* See all of your attention on *that word.* And now move forward to the word *in,* I-n. **[Pause]** See the word flashing on the inner screen of your mind. And now instantly shift back to the space between *art* and *in,* and stay right there, in silence. **[Pause]** And now Japa, in the space between your thoughts: "Ahhhhhhhhhh. Ahhhhhhhhhh."

And now shift to the word *in* on the inner screen of your mind. And now move forward, and see the word *heaven* appearing on the inner screen of your mind. *Heaven.* And now instantly shift backwards, to that space between those two words in your mind, between *in* and *heaven,* and stay right there, allowing no thoughts to penetrate. **[Pause]**

And now Japa, while in the gap, while in the space between your thoughts: "Ahhhhhhhhhh. Ahhhhhhhhhh."

And now move your thoughts, energy, to the word *heaven* and see the word *heaven* flash on the inner screen of your mind, and now move forward to the word *hallowed* and see *hallowed* appear before your mind. **[Pause]** And now, even more quickly, move back to the space between the two words *heaven* and *hallowed* in your mind, and put all of your attention on nothing more than the space between those two words, or the gap between those two thoughts. **[Pause]** And now repeat the sound of the name of God: "Ahhhhhhhhhh. Ahhhhhhhhhh."

And now move your thoughts to the word *hallowed* on the inner screen of your mind . . . and move quickly forward to the word *be*. *Hallowed, be,* and then instantly shift back from *be* to the space between *hallowed* and *be,* and put all of your energy and all of your attention on nothing more than the space between these two thoughts. You are in the gap. **[Pause]** And now Japa, while in the space between these two thoughts: "Ahhhhhhhhhh. Ahhhhhhhhhh."

And now quickly put your attention on the word *be*, b-e, and now shift forward quickly to the word *Thy* and instantly go back to the space between those two words, and reenter the gap, between the words or the thoughts *be* and *Thy*. And stay in this silent space a little bit longer each time. **[Pause]** And now we'll do Japa while in the gap. We will make conscious contact with God by repeating the sound that is in that name for God: "Ahhhhhhhhhh. Ahhhhhhhhhh."

And now instantly shift out of that gap and into the word *Thy*. And almost instantly, shift now to the word *name*. And instantly go backwards to the space between *Thy* and *name*, and rest in that space that nurtures your soul, while you're making conscious contact with God, while in the gap. **[Pause]** And now Japa, while in this . . . gap, between *Thy* and *name*: "Ahhhhhhhhhh. Ahhhhhhhhhh."

[Pause]

You have now completed a voyage through the gap, or the space between your thoughts, by using the first ten words of "The Lord's Prayer," and accessing the presence of this Divine Energy by repeating the sound of *ah*. This sound of *ah* is the only sound that you can make that requires no effort. In order to make a sound, you must move either your teeth or your tongue or your lips or your jaw, and aspirate air. But if you move nothing, and just open your mouth and let the sound come out, effortless perfection is the sound of *ah,* the sound of God, which you can practice while in the gap, at any time you choose. This technique, for me, allows my mind to get off of all of the thoughts that want to penetrate and enter into my mind. It allows me to experience the bliss, joy, fulfillment, and exquisite knowing that I am making conscious contact with God—by leaving my thoughts and entering into the space between those thoughts where all creation takes place.

Track 2 *(longer version)*

What I would like you to do first is get comfortable, close your eyes, be in any position that appeals to you—whether it's lying down or sitting up, or in a yoga position, or on your favorite chair—and put your hands very lightly on your lap, face up, with your forefinger and your thumb just barely touching each other so that you can make an imaginary circuit between the words that you are hearing, the sound that you are hearing here, and your heart.

I'm going to ask you now to put all of your attention on the word *Our,* O-u-r. Place your attention on the word *Our,* and see it appearing on the screen of your mind. **[Pause]** Now I would like you to move your attention off of the word *Our* and onto the word *Father.* See the word *Father* appearing before you. Now what I'd like you to do is slip back into the space between those two words in your mind. Go back now to the space between *Our* and *Father.* And just rest there. Now I would like you to repeat that sound of God, the sound of *ah,* Japa. While in the gap: "Ahhhhhhhhhh.

Ahhhhhhhhhh." If any thought enters your mind, return to the sound of ah. Staying in the gap between *Our* and *Father.*

Now move your attention to the word *Father* again and see *Father* appearing on the screen of your inner mind. **[Pause]** Now move forward in your mind to the word *Who,* and see the word *Who* appearing on the screen of your mind. Now instantly slip back into the gap between the words *Father* and *Who,* and put all of your attention just on this gap and nothing more. **[Pause]** And now we will do Japa: "Ahh-hhhhhhhh. Ahhhhhhhhhh."

Now, on the inner screen of your mind, see the word *Who* flash before you. W-h-o. Put all of your attention on the word *Who.* Now shift forward to the word *art.* Put all of your attention on the word *art.* Now instantly shift backwards into the space between *Who* and *art,* and stay in that space, with no thoughts penetrating. **[Pause]** Feel the lightness of the gap. **[Pause]** And now Japa: "Ahhhhhhhhhh. Ahhhhhh-hhhh."

Now shift the inner screen of your mind to the word *art.* See all of your attention on that word. And now move forward to the word *in,* I-n. **[Pause]** See the word flashing on the inner screen of your mind. And now instantly shift back to the space between *art* and *in,* and stay right there, in silence. **[Pause]** And now Japa, in the space between your thoughts: "Ahhhhhhhhhh. Ahhhhhhhhhh."

And now shift to the word *in* on the inner screen of your mind. And now move forward, and see the word *heaven* appearing on the inner screen of your mind. *Heaven.* And now instantly shift backwards, to that space between those two words in your mind, between *in* and *heaven,* and stay right there, allowing no thoughts to penetrate. **[Pause]** And now Japa, while in the gap, while in the space between your thoughts: "Ahhhhhhhhhh. Ahhhhhhhhhh."

And now move your thoughts, energy, to the word *heaven,* and see the word *heaven* flash on the inner screen of your mind, and now move forward to the word *hallowed,* and see *hallowed* appear before your mind. **[Pause]** And now, even more quickly, move back to the space between the two words, *heaven* and *hallowed* in your mind, and put all of your attention on nothing more than the space between those two words, or the gap between those two thoughts. **[Pause]** And now repeat the sound of the name of God: "Ahhhhhhhhhh. Ahhhhhhhhhh."

And now move your thoughts to the word *hallowed* on the inner screen of your mind . . . and move quickly forward to the word *be*. *Hallowed, be,* and then instantly shift back from *be* to the space between *hallowed* and *be,* and put all of your energy and all of your attention on nothing more than the space between these two thoughts. You are in the gap. **[Pause]** And now Japa, while in the space between these two thoughts: "Ahhhhhhhhhh. Ahhhhhhhhhh."

And now quickly put your attention on the word *be*, b-e, and now shift forward quickly to the word *Thy* and instantly go back to the space between those two words, and reenter the gap, between the words or the thoughts *be* and *Thy*. And stay in this silent space a little bit longer each time. **[Pause]** And now we'll do Japa while in the gap. We will make conscious contact with God by repeating the sound that is in that name for God: "Ahhhhhhhhhh. Ahhhhhhhhhh."

And now instantly shift out of that gap and into the word *Thy*. And almost instantly, shift now to the word *name*. And instantly go backwards to the space between *Thy* and *name* and rest in that space that nurtures your soul, while you're making conscious contact with God, while in the gap. **[Pause]**

And now Japa, while in this . . . gap, between *Thy* and *name*: "Ahhhhhhhhhh. Ahhhhhhhhhh."

[Pause]

You have now completed a voyage through the gap, or the space between your thoughts, by using the first ten words of "The Lord's Prayer," and accessing the presence of this Divine Energy by repeating the sound of *ah*. This sound of *ah* is the only sound that you can make that requires no effort. In order to make a sound, you must move either your teeth or your tongue or your lips or your jaw, and aspirate air. But if you move nothing, and just open your mouth and let the sound come out, effortless perfection is the sound of *ah*, the sound of God, which you can practice while in the gap, at any time you choose. This technique, for me, allows my mind to get off of all of the thoughts that want to penetrate and enter into my mind. It allows me to experience the bliss, joy, fulfillment, and exquisite knowing that I am making conscious contact with God—by leaving my thoughts and entering into the space between those thoughts where all creation takes place.

BONUS CONTENT

Thank you for purchasing *Getting in the Gap* by Wayne Dyer. This product includes a free download! To access this bonus content, please visit www.hayhouse.com/download and enter the Product ID and Download Code as they appear below.

Product ID: 132
Download Code: ebook

For further assistance, please contact Hay House Customer Care by phone: US (800) 654-5126 or INTL CC+(760) 431-7695 or visit www.hayhouse.com/contact.php.

Thank you again for your Hay House purchase. Enjoy!

GETTING IN THE GAP Audio Download Track List

1. Introduction
2. Meditation
3. Meditation (longer version)

Caution: This audio program features meditation/visualization exercises that render it inappropriate for use while driving or operating heavy machinery.

Publisher's note: Hay House products are intended to be powerful, inspirational, and life-changing tools for personal growth and healing. They are not intended as a substitute for medical care. Please use this audio program under the supervision of your care provider. Neither the author nor Hay House, Inc., assumes any responsibility for your improper use of this product.

ABOUT THE AUTHOR

Affectionately called the 'father of motivation' by his fans, **Dr Wayne W. Dyer** was an internationally renowned author, speaker and pioneer in the field of self-development. Over the four decades of his career he wrote more than 40 books, including *Manifest Your Destiny, Wisdom of the Ages, There's a Spiritual Solution to Every Problem* and the *New York Times* bestsellers *10 Secrets for Success and Inner Peace, The Power of Intention, Inspiration, Change Your Thoughts – Change Your Life, Excuses Begone!, Wishes Fulfilled* and *I Can See Clearly Now*. He also created numerous audio programmes and videos, and appeared on thousands of radio and television shows, including *The Today Show, The Tonight Show* and *Oprah*.

Wayne held a doctorate in educational counselling from Wayne State University, was an associate professor at St. John's University in New York and honoured a lifetime commitment to education and finding the Higher Self. In 2015 he left his body, returning to Infinite Source to embark on his next adventure.

www.drwaynedyer.com

Hay House Titles
of Related Interest

Books

Chakra Clearing, by Doreen Virtue, Ph.D.

Contacting Your Spirit Guide,
by Sylvia Browne (book and CD)

The Journey to the Sacred Garden,
by Hank Wesselman, Ph.D. (book and CD)

Meditation, by Brian Weiss, M.D. (book and CD)

Meditations to Heal Your Life,
by Louise L. Hay

Power vs. Force,
by David R. Hawkins, M.D., Ph.D.

Reclaim Your Spiritual Power,
by Ron Roth, Ph.D., with Peter Occhiogrosso

7 Paths to God, by Joan Borysenko, Ph.D.

Audio Programs

The Art of Meditation, by Stuart Wilde

Complete Relaxation, by Denise Linn

Healing Journey, by Emmett E. Miller, M.D.

The Yoga of Love and Devotion,
a Dialogue Between Shree Maa and Deepak Chopra, M.D.

All of the above are available at your local bookstore,
or may be ordered through Hay House, Inc.:

(800) 654-5126 or **(760) 431-7695**
(800) 650-5115 (fax) or **(760) 431-6948 (fax)**
www.hayhouse.com

❧ NOTES ❧

❧ NOTES ❧

❦ NOTES ❦

❧ NOTES ❧

NOTES

❦ NOTES ❦

HAY HOUSE

Look within

Join the conversation about latest products, events, exclusive offers and more.

f   Hay House UK

🐦   @HayHouseUK

📷   @hayhouseuk

♥   healyourlife.com

We'd love to hear from you!